Quick and Easy Air Fryer Recipes Cookbook

Quick, Healthy, Easy And Delicious Recipes For the whole family

Nichole S. Rodriguez

TABLE OF CONTENTS

INTRODUCTION

The secret of Air Fryer is the unique cooking technology that uses hot-air that circulates inside the fryer. It works no different than any other thermic-processing method, but without all the detrimental side-effects you get when you eat deep-fried foods, for example. You may be able not only to fry but also to bake, broil, roast, rotisserie, and steam things as well. Air Fryer can also be a great substitute for your microwave, oven, or a stove. Except it's much healthier, easier, and faster to use.

On top of that, you can use an air fryer to prepare batters and marinades. The only thing that you should never put in there is generally speaking liquids. That means that things like broth or other soups are not coming at play here. Remember, safety comes first. But given the wide variety of other things you can do with it - it's a tiny con.

Air fryer benefits

Almost no fat and oil involved

Probably the biggest benefit of using the Air Fryer is reducing the amount of oil or other fats you normally use to cook your meals. With the help of Air Fryer as much as one tablespoon is enough to gain the same effect as if you were cooking regular deep fried fries or spring rolls. As hot air circulates inside of the chamber, it makes the food crispy on the outside and tender on the inside.

Fewer calories

Needless to say, as you reduce the amount of fat in your meals, their calorific value drops as well. So not only you eat overall healthier but even your "cheat meals" are less of a problem now. As you can see, using an air fryer can effectively help you drop some extra weight. Maybe it's time you reinstated your relationship with French fries?

It's compact, and it fits everywhere

Because it takes so little space on the kitchen countertop, you don't have to worry about additional clutter. It also doesn't kill the aesthetics of your countertop. You can also put all the accessories inside the fryer, so you reduce unnecessary mess to a 0 level. See how you can start enjoying being in the kitchen again.

How to use an air fryer?

Prepare the air fryer

Some recipes will require using a basket, a rack, or a rotisserie. Some other recipes require cake or muffin pans. Before you pick the recipe and prepare your accessories, make sure they fit into your fryer.

Prepare the ingredients

Once you have all that's necessary to prepare your recipe, place the ingredients directly inside the appliance or use a basket, a rack, or a pan to do so. To prevent sticking use parchment baking paper or simply spray the food with a little bit of oil. A word of caution is necessary here. Never over-stuff the chamber with too much food. It will not cook to an equal measure, and you may find yourself getting frustrated chewing under-cooked bits. If you're planning on cooking more, multiple rounds of air-frying may be necessary.

Set the temperature and time

Most of Air Fryers use pre-set modes depending on the type of recipe. You can adjust settings such as time and temperature manually to make the best use of your recipes.

Cleaning time

Before you start cleaning, plug the air fryer off and let it cool down. Once it's ready, stick to instructions you got from the manufacturer and never scrub or use any other abrasive material on the inner surface of the chamber.

Air fryer recipes

Keep an eye on timing

You may discover that different models cook at different temperatures.

2. Quiche Muffin Cups

Preparation time: 8 minutes

Cooking Time: 14 minutes

Servings: 10

Ingredients:

- ¼ pound all-natural ground pork sausage

- 3 eggs

- ¾ cup milk

- 4 ounces sharp Cheddar cheese, grated

- 1 muffin pan

- Cooking spray

Directions:

1. On a clean work surface, slice the pork sausage into 2-ounce portions. Shape each portion into a ball and gently flatten it with your palm.

2. Lay the patties in the air fryer basket and cook in the preheated instant pot at 375°F for 6 minutes. Flip the patties over when the lid screen indicates 'TURN FOOD' during cooking time.

3. Meanwhile, whisk the eggs and milk in a bowl, and stir until creamy. Set aside.

4. Remove the patties from the basket to a large dish lined with paper towels. Crumble them into small pieces with a fork. Set aside.

5. Line a muffin pan with 10 paper liners. Lightly spray the muffin cups with cooking spray.

6. Divide crumbled sausage equally among the 10 muffin cups and sprinkle the tops with the cheese.

7. Arrange the muffin pan in air fryer basket. Pour the egg mixture into the muffin cups, filling each about three-quarters full.

8. Put the air fryer lid on and cook in the preheated instant pot at 375°F for 8 minutes, until the tops are golden and a toothpick inserted in the middle comes out clean.

9. Remove from the basket and let cool for 5 minutes before serving.

Nutrition: Calories: 497, Total Fat: 25g, Saturated Fat: 2g, Total Carbs: 1g, Fiber: 4g, Protein: 28g,

3. <u>Vegetable and Ham Omelet</u>

Preparation time: 5 minutes

Cooking Time: 20minutes

Servings: 6

Ingredients:

- ¼ cup ham, diced

- ¼ cup green or red bell pepper, cored and chopped

- ¼ cup onion, chopped

- 1 teaspoon butter

- 4 large eggs

- 2 tablespoons milk

- 1/8 teaspoon salt

- ¾ cup sharp Cheddar cheese, grated

Directions:

1. Add the ham, bell pepper, onion, and butter into a 6×6×2-inch baking pan. Place the pan inside the air fryer basket.

2. Put the air fryer lid on and cook in the preheated instant pot at 375°F for 6 minutes. Stir once halfway through the cooking time, or until the vegetables are soft.

3. In a bowl, whisk the eggs, milk, and salt until smooth and creamy. Gently pour over the ham and vegetables in the pan.

4. Put the air fryer lid on and cook at 375°F for about 13 minutes, or until the top begins to turn brown.

5. Top with the cheese and cook for 1 minute more, or until the cheese is bubbly and melted.

6. Remove from the basket and cool for 5 minutes before serving.

Nutrition: Calories: 367, Total Fat: 14g, Saturated Fat: 5g, Total Carbs: 13g, Fiber: 6g, Protein: 18g,

4. Cheesy Canadian Bacon English Muffin

Preparation time: 7 minutes

Cooking Time: 8 minutes

Servings: 4

Ingredients:

- 4 English muffins

- 8 slices Canadian bacon

- 4 slices cheese

- Cooking spray

Directions:

1. On a clean work surface, cut each English muffin in half.

2. To assemble a sandwich, layer 2 slices of bacon and 1 cheese slice on the bottom of each muffin and put the other half of the muffin on top. Repeat with remaining muffins, bacon, and cheese slices.

3. Arrange the sandwiches in the air fryer basket and spritz with cooking spray. You may need to work in batches to avoid overcrowding.

4. Put the air fryer lid on and cook in the preheated instant pot at 375°F for 8 minutes. Flip the sandwiches when it shows 'TURN FOOD' on the air fryer lid screen during cooking time.

5. Transfer to a plate and repeat with remaining sandwiches.

6. Let them cool for 3 minutes before serving.

Nutrition: Calories: 322, Total Fat: 15g, Saturated Fat: 8g, Cholesterol: 58mg, Sodium: 119mg, Carbohydrates: 27g, Fiber: 4g, Protein: 24g

5. Asparagus, Cheese and Egg Strata

Preparation time: 6 minutes

Cooking Time: 19 minutes

Servings: 4

Ingredients:

- 6 asparagus spears, cut into 2-inch pieces

- ½ cup grated Havarti or Swiss cheese

- 4 eggs

- 2 slices whole-wheat bread, cut into ½-inch cubes

- 3 tablespoons whole milk

- 2 tablespoons flat-leaf parsley, chopped

- 1 tablespoon water

- Freshly ground black pepper and salt to taste

- Cooking spray

Directions:

1. Place a 6×6×2-inch baking pan into the air fryer basket. Add 1 tablespoon water and asparagus spears into the pan.

2. Put the air fryer lid on and cook in the preheated instant pot at 325°F for 3 to 5 minutes, or until the asparagus spears are tender.

3. Remove the asparagus spears from the baking pan. Drain and dry them thoroughly. Place the asparagus spears and bread cubes in the pan, then spray with cooking spray. Set aside.

4. In a bowl, whisk the eggs and milk together. Add the cheese, parsley, salt and pepper. Stir to combine. Pour the mixture into the pan and place the pan into the air fryer basket.

5. Put the air fryer lid on and bake at 350°F for 11 to 14 minutes, or until a knife inserted in the center comes out clean.

6. Remove the strata from the pan. Let cool for 5 minutes before serving.

Nutrition: Calories: 1214, Total Fat: 90.11g, Saturated Fat: 29.721g, Total Carbs: 6.16g, Fiber: 0.4g, Protein: 32.73g,

6. <u>Shrimp, Spinach and Rice Frittata</u>

Preparation time: 12 minutes

Cooking Time: 18 minutes

Servings: 4

Ingredients:

- ½ cup chopped shrimp, cooked

- ½ cup baby spinach

- ½ cup rice, cooked

- 4 eggs

- ½ cup grated Monterey Jack cheese

- ½ teaspoon dried basil

- Pinch salt

- Cooking spray

Directions:

1. In a bowl, whisk together the eggs, basil and salt.

2. Spritz a 6×6×2-inch baking pan with cooking spray. Place the cooked shrimp, rice and spinach into the pan, and stir to combine well. Pour in the egg mixture and sprinkle the cheese on top. Put the pan into the air fryer basket.

3. Put the air fryer lid on and bake in the preheated instant pot at 325°F for 14 to 18 minutes, or until puffy and golden brown.

4. Remove from the pan and cool for 3 minutes before cutting into wedges to serve.

Nutrition: Calories: 1358, Total Fat: 81.86g, Saturated Fat: 29.089g, Total Carbs: 8.86g, Fiber: 3.1g, Protein: 35.54g,

7. Tender Monkey Bread with Cinnamon

Preparation time: 6 minutes

Cooking Time: 9 minutes

Servings: 4

Ingredients:

- 1 can (8-ounce) refrigerated biscuits

- 3 tablespoons brown sugar

- ¼ cup white sugar

- ½ teaspoon cinnamon

- 1/8 teaspoon nutmeg

- 3 tablespoons unsalted butter, melted

Directions:

1. On your cutting board, divide each biscuit into quarters.

2. In a mixing bowl, add the brown and white sugar, nutmeg, and cinnamon. Stir well.

3. Pour the melted butter into a medium bowl. Dip each biscuit in the melted butter, then in the sugar mixture to coat well.

4. Arrange the coated biscuits in a 6×6×2-inch baking pan and place the pan into the air fryer basket.

5. Put the air fryer lid on and bake in batches in the preheated instant pot at 350°F for 6 to 9 minutes until set.

6. Transfer to a serving dish and cool for 5 minutes before serving.

Nutrition: Calories: 1228, Total Fat: 42.64g, Total Carbs: 31.53g, Fiber: 1.2g, Protein: 49.97g,

8. Grilled Ham and Cheese Sandwiches

Preparation time: 7 minutes

Cooking Time: 8 minutes

Servings: 2

Ingredients:

- 4 slices smoked country ham

- 4 slices Cheddar cheese

- 4 slices bread

- 4 thick slices tomato

- 1 teaspoon butter

Directions:

1. Spread one side of 2 slices of bread with ½ teaspoon of butter.

2. To assemble a sandwich, layer 2 slices of ham, 2 slices of cheese and 2 slices of tomato onto the unbuttered sides of bread slices. Then arrange the other bread slices (buttered side up) on top.

3. Place the sandwiches (buttered side down) in the air fryer basket.

4. Put the air fryer lid on and cook in the preheated instant pot at 375°F for 8 minutes. Flip the sandwiches when it shows 'TURN FOOD' on the air fryer lid screen during cooking time.

5. Transfer to a serving dish and enjoy.

Nutrition: Calories: 246, Total Fat: 11g, Saturated Fat: 14g, Cholesterol: 88mg, Sodium: 1618mg, Carbohydrates: 22g, Fiber: 3g, Protein: 17g

9. Pesto Cheese Gnocchi

Preparation time: 11 minutes

Cooking Time: 16 minutes **Servings:** 4

Ingredients:

- 1 jar (8-ounce) pesto

- 1/3 cup Parmesan cheese, grated

- 1 package (16-ounce) shelf-stable gnocchi

- 1 onion, finely chopped

- 3 cloves garlic, sliced

- 1 tablespoon olive oil

Directions:

1. Mix the oil, onion, garlic, and gnocchi in a 6×6×2-inch baking pan. Place the pan into the air fryer basket. Put the air fryer lid on and bake in the preheated instant pot at 400°F for 16 minutes, or until the gnocchi starts to brown. Stir once halfway through cooking time. Transfer the gnocchi to a serving dish. Sprinkle with the Parmesan cheese and pesto. Stir well and serve warm. **Nutrition:** Calories: 1382, Total Fat: 48.35g, Saturated Fat: 15.423g, Total Carbs: 83.21g,

MAIN DISH

10. Mini Lava Cake

Preparation time: 10 minutes

Cooking time: 20 minutes

Servings: 3

Ingredients:

- 1 egg

- 4 tablespoon. sugar

- 2 tablespoon. olive oil

- 4 tablespoon. milk

- 4 tablespoon. flour

- 1 tablespoon cocoa powder

- ½ teaspoon. baking powder

- ½ teaspoon. orange zest

Directions:

1. In a bowl, mix egg with sugar, oil, milk, flour, salt, cocoa powder, baking powder and orange zest, stir very well and pour this into greased ramekins.

2. Add ramekins to your air fryer and cook at 320 °F for 20minutes.

3. Serve lava cakes warm.

Nutrition: Calories: 227; Fat: 8g; Protein: 5.6g

11. Easy Air Fried Meatballs

Preparation time: 10 minutes

Cooking time: 8 minutes

Servings: 4

Ingredients:

- 1½ cups of ground beef

- 1½ ounce of breadcrumbs

- 1 egg

- 1 small sized onion, finely chopped

- 3 teaspoons. of parsley, chopped

- 2 teaspoons. of fresh thyme, chopped

- Salt and pepper to taste

Directions:

1. Mix the onions, parsley, beef, breadcrumbs, egg, thyme, salt and pepper in a bowl. Mold the mixture into 12 balls.

2. Heat your air fryer to 390°F and put the balls into the fryer basket. Cook the meatballs for 8 minutes.

3. Serve the meatballs with ketchup or your favorite ketchup.

Nutrition: Calories: 432; Fat: 14g; Protein: 29g

12. <u>Battered & Crispy Fish Tacos</u>

Preparation time: 10 minutes

Cooking time: 10 minutes

Servings: 2

Ingredients:

- 1 1/2 cup Flour Corn

- Tortillas Peach Salsa Cilantro

- Fresh halibut, slice into strips

- 1 can of beer

- 2 tablespoon. Vegetable Oil

- 1 teaspoon. baking powder

- 1 teaspoon. Salt Cholula sauce Avocado Cream (recipe below)

Directions:

1. Lay out the corn tortillas topped with peach salsa on a plate and set aside.

2. Combine 1 cup of flour, beer and baking powder until it forms a pancake like consistency.

3. Toss the fish in the remaining flour then dip in the beer batter mixture until well coated.

4. Place on preheated air fryer rack and cook 6-8 minutes or until golden at 200°F.

5. Place the fish on top of the salsa mixture topped with avocado cream, cilantro and Cholula sauce.

6. To Make the Avocado Cream: 1 large avocado 3/4 cup margarine milk Juice from 1/2 lime Combine in a blender until smooth.

Nutrition: Calories: 299; Fat: 17g; Protein: 29g

13. Steamed Salmon & Dill Dip

Preparation time: 15 minutes

Cooking time: 10 minutes **Servings:** 2

Ingredients:

- ¾ pound of salmon, cut in half

- 8 tablespoon. of sour cream

- 2 teaspoons. of olive oil

- 6 teaspoons. of finely chopped dill

- 8 tablespoon. of Greek Yogurt

- ¼ teaspoons. of salt

Directions:

1. Heat your air fryer to 285°F. Add a cup of cool water at the base of your air fryer. Coat each portion of the salmon with olive oil and season with salt. Place into the fryer basket and cook for about 11 minutes. While cooking the fish, mix the sour cream, salt, yogurt and dill in a bowl. Remove the fish from the air fryer and garnish with a pinch of dill and serve with the dill dip.

Nutrition: Calories: 539; Fat: 17g; Protein: 30g

14. Famous Cheese and Bacon Rolls

Preparation time: 10 minutes

Cooking time: 10 minutes

Servings: 6

Ingredients:

- 1/3 cup Swiss cheese, shredded 10 slices of bacon

- 10 ounces canned crescent rolls

- 2 tablespoon. yellow mustard 6

Directions:

1. Start by preheating your air fryer to 325 °F.

2. Then, form the crescent rolls into "sheets". Spread mustard over the sheets. Place the chopped Swiss cheese and bacon in the middle of each dough sheet.

3. Create the rolls and bake them for about 9 minutes.

4. Then, set the machine to 385 °F; bake for an additional 4 minutes in the preheated air fryer. Eat warm with some extra yellow mustard.

Nutrition: Calories: 109; Fat: 2g; Protein: 32g

15. Baked Eggs with Kale and Ham

Preparation time: 15 minutes

Cooking time: 10 minutes

Servings: 2

Ingredients

- 2 eggs

- 1/4 teaspoon. dried or fresh marjoram 2 teaspoons. chili powder

- 1/3 teaspoon. kosher salt

- ½ cup steamed kale

- 1/4 teaspoon. dried or fresh rosemary 4 Pancetta ham slices

- 1/3 teaspoon. ground black pepper, or more to taste

Directions:

1. Divide the kale and ham among 2 ramekins; crack an egg into each ramekin. Sprinkle with seasonings.

2. Cook for 15 minutes at 335 °F or until your eggs reach desired texture.

3. Serve warm with spicy tomato ketchup and pickles.

Nutrition: Calories: 159; Fat: 16g; Protein: 21.6g

16. Easiest Pancetta Chops Ever

Preparation time: 10 minutes

Cooking time: 12 minutes

Servings: 6

Ingredients:

- 1/3 cup Italian breadcrumbs

- Roughly chopped fresh cilantro, to taste 2 teaspoons. Cajun seasonings

- Nonstick cooking spray 2 eggs, beaten

- 3 tablespoon. white flour

- 1 teaspoon. seasoned salt

- Garlic & onion spice blend, to taste 6 Pancetta chops

- 1/3 teaspoon. freshly cracked black pepper

Directions:

1. Coat the Pancetta chops with Cajun seasonings, salt, pepper, and the spice blend on all sides.

2. Then, add the flour to a plate. In a shallow dish, whisk the egg until pale and smooth. Place the Italian breadcrumbs in the third bowl.

3. Dredge each Pancetta piece in the flour; then, coat them with the egg; finally, coat them with the breadcrumbs. Spritz them with cooking spray on both sides.

4. Now, air-fry Pancetta chops for about 18 minutes at 345 °F; make sure to taste for doneness after first 12 minutes of cooking. Lastly, garnish with fresh cilantro.

Nutrition: Calories: 459; Fat: 22g; Protein:26g

17. Onion Rings Wrapped in Bacon

Preparation time: 10 minutes

Cooking time: 15 minutes

Servings: 4

Ingredients:

- 12 rashers back bacon

- 1/2 teaspoon. ground black pepper Chopped fresh parsley, to taste 1/2 teaspoon. paprika

- 1/2 teaspoon. chili powder 1/2 tablespoon soy sauce

- ½ teaspoon. salt

Directions:

1. Start by preheating your air fryer to 355 °F.

2. Season the onion rings with paprika, salt, black pepper, and chili powder. Simply wrap the bacon around the onion rings; drizzle with soy sauce.

3. Bake for 17 minutes, garnish with fresh parsley and serve.

Nutrition: Calories: 219; Fat: 10g; Protein:15.6g

SIDE DISHES

18. Air Fried Ratatouille

Preparation time: 25 minutes

Cooking time: 25 minutes

Servings: 4

Ingredients:

- Zucchini, diced into cubes – 1

- Eggplant, small diced into cubes - ½

- Tomato, chopped into cubed – 1 medium

- Red bell pepper, chopped - ½ large

- Onion, cut into cubes - ½

- Cayenne pepper, fresh, chopped – 1

- Vinegar – 1 teaspoon

- Garlic clove, grated – 1

- Fresh basil, stemmed and chopped – 5 springs

- Fresh oregano, stemmed and cut into pieces – 2 springs

- Olive oil – 1 tablespoon

- White wine – 1 tablespoon

- Salt – to taste

- Pepper - ½ teaspoon

Directions:

1. Put zucchini, eggplant, bell peppers, tomato, onion in bowl and mix.

2. After that, you can add basil, garlic, cayenne pepper, oregano, pepper, and salt. Mix all the ingredients.

3. Now pour vinegar, oil, and wine to the mix and let it coat evenly on the vegetables.

4. Preheat the air fryer at 200 degrees Celsius before you start the cooking.

5. Now transfer the vegetable mix into a baking dish and put in the air fryer basket.Start cooking for 8 minutes and stir it.

6. Again, cook for another 8 minutes and stir. It would be better if you can stir it every 5 minutes and cook for a total of 25-30 minutes.

7. After cooking keep the dish in the air fryer for some time.

8. Serve hot.

Nutrition: Calories: 79 Carbohydrate: 10.2g Cholesterol: 0mg Dietary Fiber: 3.3g Sodium: 48mg Protein: 2.1g Sugars: 5g

19. Air Fryer Rosemary Potato Wedges

Preparation time: 10 minutes

Cooking time: 20 minutes

Servings: 4

Ingredients:

- Potatoes – 2

- Fresh rosemary, chopped – 1 tablespoon

- Olive oil – 1 tablespoon

- Salt – 2 tablespoons

Directions:

1. Wash, clean and slice the potatoes in 12 wedges with skin.

2. Put the potatoes in a large vessel.

3. Drizzle olive oil over it and toss.

4. Sprinkle chopped rosemary, salt and toss it to mix the ingredients.

5. Preheat the air fryer at 190 degrees Celsius before you start cooking.

6. When the air fryer is hot, layer the potato wedges in the air fryer basked without crowding or overlapping.

7. Air fry it for 10 minutes and flip the wedges by using a tong and continue cooking for another 10 minutes.

8. If your air fryer basket is too small, you need to cook it in batches.

9. Serve hot.

Nutrition: Calories: 115 Carbohydrates: 19.2g Cholesterol: 0mg Dietary Fiber: 2.5g Protein: 2.2g Sugars: 1g Sodium: 465mg Fat: 1.0g

20. Air Fried Asparagus

Preparation Time: 5 minutes

Cooking Time: 10 minutes

Servings: 4

Ingredients:

- Asparagus - ½ bunch

- Salt - ¼ teaspoon

- Black pepper - ½ teaspoon

- Olive oil spray – as required

Directions:

1. Cut and remove 2" from the bottom portion of asparagus.

2. Place the asparagus sticks in the air fryer basket.

3. Spray coat olive oil on it.

4. Sprinkle the black pepper powder.

5. Set the temperature to 200 degrees Celsius and timer for 10 minutes.

6. Serve hot.

Nutrition: Calories: 11 Carbohydrates: 0.2g Cholesterol: 0mg Sodium: 147mg Dietary Fiber: 0.1g Sugars: 0g

SEAFOOD RECIPES

21. Oaty Fishcakes

Preparation time: 5 minutes

Cooking time: 15 minutes

Servings: 4

Ingredients:

- 4 potatoes, cooked and mashed

- 2 salmon fillets, cubed

- 1 haddock fillet, cubed

- 1 teaspoon Dijon mustard

- ½ cup oats

- 2 tablespoon. fresh dill, chopped

- 2 tablespoon. olive oil

- Salt and black pepper to taste

Directions:

1. Preheat air fryer to 400 F. Boil salmon and haddock cubes in a pot filled with salted water over medium heat for 5 minutes.

2. Drain, cool, and pat dry. Flake or shred and add to a bowl. Mix in mashed potatoes, mustard, oats, dill, salt, and pepper.

3. Shape into balls and flatten to make patties. Brush with olive oil and arrange them on the bottom of the frying basket.

4. Bake for 10 minutes, flipping once halfway through. Let cool before serving.

Nutrition: Calories: 435; fat: 10g; Carbohydrates:37g; Protein: 14g

22. Barramundi Fillets in Lemon Sauce

Preparation time: 5 minutes

Cooking time: 20 minutes

Servings: 4

Ingredients:

- 4 barramundi fillets

- 1 lemon, juiced

- Salt and black pepper to taste

- 2 tablespoon. butter

- ½ cup white wine

- 8 black peppercorns

- 2 cloves garlic, minced

- 2 shallots, chopped

Directions:

1. Preheat air fryer to 390 F. Season the fillets and place them inside the greased air fryer basket.

2. Air Fry for 15 minutes, flipping once halfway through until the edges are golden brown. Remove to a plate.

3. Melt the butter in a pan over low heat. Add in garlic and shallots and stir-fry for 3 minutes. Pour in white wine, lemon juice, and peppercorns.

4. Cook until the liquid is reduced by three quarters, about 3-5 minutes. Adjust the seasoning and strain the sauce. Drizzle the sauce over the fish and serve.

Nutrition: Calories: 200; fat: 6g; Carbohydrates: 23g; Protein: 15g

23. Greek-Style Salmon with Dill Sauce

Preparation time: 10 minutes

Cooking time: 10 minutes

Servings: 4

Ingredients:

- 1-pound salmon fillets

- Salt and black pepper to taste

- 2 teaspoon olive oil

- 2 tablespoon. fresh dill, chopped

- 1 cup sour cream

- 1 cup Greek yogurt

Directions:

1. In a bowl, mix sour cream, yogurt, dill, and salt; set aside.

2. Preheat air fryer to 340 F. Drizzle olive oil over the salmon and rub with salt and black pepper.

3. Arrange the fish in the frying basket and Bake for 10 minutes, flipping once. Top with the yogurt sauce.

Nutrition: Calories: 409; fat: 8g; Carbohydrates: 30g; Protein: 43g

24. Kimchi-Spiced Salmon

Preparation time: 5 minutes

Cooking time: 10 minutes

Servings: 4

Ingredients:

- 2 tablespoon. soy sauce

- 2 tablespoon. sesame oil

- 2 tablespoon. mirin

- 2 tablespoon. ginger puree

- 1 teaspoon kimchi spice

- 1 teaspoon sriracha sauce

- 2 pounds' salmon fillets

- 1 lime, cut into wedges

Directions:

1. Preheat air fryer to 350 F. Grease the air fryer basket with cooking spray. In a bowl, mix together soy sauce, mirin, ginger puree, kimchi spice, and sriracha sauce.

2. Add the salmon fillets and toss to coat.

3. Place in the air fryer basket and drizzle with sesame oil. Air Fry for 10 minutes, flipping once halfway through. Garnish with lime wedges and serve.

Nutrition: Calories: 420; fat: 11g; Carbohydrates: 12g; Protein: 13g

POULTRY RECIPES

25. Air Fryer Chicken Parmesan

Preparation time: 15 minutes

Cooking time: 9 minutes

Servings: 4

Ingredients:

- ½ C. keto marinara

- 6 tablespoon. mozzarella cheese

- 1 tablespoon. melted ghee

- 2 tablespoon. grated parmesan cheese

- 6 tablespoon. gluten-free seasoned breadcrumbs

- 2 8-ounce chicken breasts

Directions:

1. Ensure air fryer is preheated to 360 degrees. Spray the basket with olive oil.

2. Mix parmesan cheese and breadcrumbs together. Melt ghee.

3. Brush melted ghee onto the chicken and dip into breadcrumb mixture.

4. Place coated chicken in the air fryer and top with olive oil.

5. Cook 2 breasts for 6 minutes and top each breast with a tablespoon of sauce and 1 ½ tablespoons of mozzarella cheese. Cook another 3 minutes to melt cheese.

6. Keep cooked pieces warm as you repeat the process with remaining breasts.

Nutrition: Calories: 251 Fat: 10g Protein: 31g Sugar: 0g

26. Jerk Chicken Wings

Preparation time: 10 minutes

Cooking time: 16 minutes

Servings: 8

Ingredients:

- 1 teaspoon. salt

- ½ C. red wine vinegar

- 5 tablespoon. lime juice

- 4 chopped scallions

- 1 tablespoon. grated ginger

- 2 tablespoon. brown sugar

- 1 tablespoon. chopped thyme

- 1 teaspoon. white pepper

- 1 teaspoon. cayenne pepper

- 1 teaspoon. cinnamon

- 1 tablespoon. allspice

- 1 Habanero pepper (seeds/ribs removed and chopped finely)

- 6 chopped garlic cloves

- 2 tablespoon. low-sodium soy sauce

- 2 tablespoon. olive oil

- 4 pounds of chicken wings

Directions:

1. Combine all ingredients except wings in a bowl. Pour into a gallon bag and add chicken wings. Chill 2-24 hours to marinate.

2. Ensure your air fryer is preheated to 390 degrees.

3. Place chicken wings into a strainer to drain excess liquids.

4. Pour half of the wings into your air fryer and cook 14-16 minutes, making sure to shake halfway through the cooking process.

5. Remove and repeat the process with remaining wings.

Nutrition: Calories: 374 Fat: 14g Protein: 33g Sugar: 4g

MEAT RECIPES

27. Balsamic Glazed Pork Chops

Preparation Time: 5 Minutes

Cooking Time: 50 Minutes

Servings: 4

Ingredients:

- ¾ cup balsamic vinegar

- 1 ½ tablespoons sugar

- 1 tablespoon butter

- tablespoons olive oil

- 3 tablespoons salt

- 3 pork rib chops

Directions:

1. Place all ingredients in bowl and allow the meat to marinate in the fridge for at least 2 hours.

2. Preheat the Smart Air Fryer Oven to 390°F.

3. Place the grill pan accessory in the air fryer.

4. Grill the pork chops for 20 minutes making sure to flip the meat every 10 minutes for even grilling.

5. Meanwhile, pour the balsamic vinegar on a saucepan and allow to simmer for at least 10 minutes until the sauce thickens.

6. Brush the meat with the glaze before serving.

Nutrition: Calories: 274; Fat: 18g; Protein:17g

28. Rustic Pork Ribs

Preparation Time: 5 Minutes

Cooking Time: 15 Minutes

Servings: 4

Ingredients:

- 1 rack of pork ribs

- tablespoons dry red wine

- 1 tablespoon soy sauce

- 1/2 teaspoon dried thyme

- 1/2 teaspoon onion powder

- 1/2 teaspoon garlic powder

- 1/2 teaspoon ground black pepper

- 1 teaspoon smoke salt

- 1 tablespoon cornstarch

- 1/2 teaspoon olive oil

Directions:

1. Begin by preheating your Smart Air Fryer Oven to 390 degrees F. Place all ingredients in a mixing bowl and let them marinate at least 1 hour.

2. Pour into the Oven rack/basket. Place the Rack on the middle-shelf of the Smart Air Fryer Oven. Set temperature to 390°F, and set time to 25 minutes. Cook the marinated ribs approximately 25 minutes.

3. Serve hot.

Nutrition: calories 131 fat 14g carbs 20g protein 21g

29. Keto Parmesan Crusted Pork Chops

Preparation Time: 10 Minutes

Cooking Time: 15 Minutes

Servings: 8

Ingredients:

- tablespoon. grated parmesan cheese

- 1 C. pork rind crumbs

- 2 beaten eggs

- ¼ teaspoon. chili powder

- ½ teaspoon. onion powder

- 1 teaspoon. smoked paprika

- ¼ teaspoon. pepper

- ½ teaspoon. salt

- 4-6 thick boneless pork chops

Directions:

1. Ensure your Smart Air Fryer Oven is preheated to 400 degrees.

2. With pepper and salt, season both sides of pork chops.

3. In a food processor, pulse pork rinds into crumbs. Mix crumbs with other seasonings. Beat eggs and add to another bowl.

4. Dip pork chops into eggs then into pork rind crumb mixture.

5. Spray down air fryer with olive oil and add pork chops to the basket. Set temperature to 400°F, and set time to 15 minutes.

Nutrition: Calories: 422; Fat: 19g; Protein:38g; Sugar:2g

30. Crispy Fried Pork Chops the Southern Way

Preparation Time: 10 Minutes

Cooking Time: 25 Minutes

Servings: 4

Ingredients:

- ½ cup all-purpose flour

- ½ cup low fat buttermilk

- ½ teaspoon black pepper

- ½ teaspoon Tabasco sauce

- teaspoon paprika

- bone-in pork chops

Directions:

1. Place the buttermilk and hot sauce in a Ziploc bag and add the pork chops. Allow to marinate for at least an hour in the fridge.

2. In a bowl, combine the flour, paprika, and black pepper.

3. Remove pork from the Ziploc bag and dredge in the flour mixture.

4. Preheat the Smart Air Fryer Oven to 390°F.

5. Spray the pork chops with cooking oil.

6. Pour into the Oven rack/basket. Place the Rack on the middle-shelf of the Smart Air Fryer Oven. Set temperature to 390°F, and set time to 25 minutes.

Nutrition: Calories: 427; Fat: 21.2g; Protein:46.4g; Sugar:2g

31. Fried Pork Quesadilla

Preparation Time: 10 Minutes

Cooking Time: 12 Minutes

Servings: 2

Ingredients:

- Two 6-inch corn or flour tortilla shells

- 1 medium-sized pork shoulder, approximately 4 ounces, sliced

- ½ medium-sized white onion, sliced

- ½ medium-sized red pepper, sliced

- ½ medium sized green pepper, sliced

- ½ medium sized yellow pepper, sliced

- ¼ cup of shredded pepper-jack cheese

- ¼ cup of shredded mozzarella cheese

Directions:

1. Preheat the Smart Air Fryer Oven to 350 degrees.

2. In the oven on high heat for 20 minutes, grill the pork, onion, and peppers in foil in the same pan, allowing the

moisture from the vegetables and the juice from the pork mingle together.

3. Remove pork and vegetables in foil from the oven. While they're cooling, sprinkle half the shredded cheese over one of the tortillas, then cover with the pieces of pork, onions, and peppers, and then layer on the rest of the shredded cheese.

4. Top with the second tortilla. Place directly on hot surface of the air fryer basket. Set the air fryer timer for 6 minutes. After 6 minutes, when the air fryer shuts off, flip the tortillas onto the other side with a spatula; the cheese should be melted enough that it won't fall apart, but be careful anyway not to spill any toppings! Reset the air fryer to 350 degrees for another 6 minutes.

5. After 6 minutes, when the air fryer shuts off, the tortillas should be browned and crisp, and the pork, onion, peppers and cheese will be crispy and hot and delicious.

6. Remove with tongs and let sit on a serving plate to cool for a few minutes before slicing.

Nutrition: Calories: 427; Fat: 21.2g; Protein:26.4g; Sugar:2g

VEGETABLE RECIPES

32. Air Fried Bananas

Preparation time: 5 minutes

Cooking time: 10 Minutes **Servings:** 4

Ingredients:

- 3 tablespoon. butter

- 2 eggs

- 8 bananas

- ½ cup corn flour

- 3 tablespoon. cinnamon sugar

- 1 cup panko

Directions:

1. Warm up pan with the butter over medium heat, put panko, turn and cook for 4 minutes then move to a bowl. Spin each in flour, panko, egg blend, assemble them in air fryer's basket, grime with cinnamon sugar and cook at 280° F for 10 minutes. Serve immediately.

Nutrition: Calories: 337 Total Fat: 3g Total carbs: 23g

33. Cocoa Cake

Preparation time: 5 minutes

Cooking time: 17 Minutes

Servings: 6

Ingredients

- oz. butter

- 3 eggs

- 3 oz. sugar

- 1 tablespoon. cocoa powder

- 3 oz. flour

- ½ tablespoon. lemon juice

Directions:

1. Mix in 1 tablespoon butter with cocoa powder in a bowl and beat.

2. Mix in the rest of the butter with eggs, flour, sugar and lemon juice in another bowl, blend properly and move half into a cake pan

3. Put half of the cocoa blend, spread, add the rest of the butter layer and crest with remaining cocoa.

4. Put into air fryer and cook at 360° F for 17 minutes.

5. Allow to cool before slicing.

6. Serve.

Nutrition: Calories: 221 Total Fat: 5g Total carbs: 12g

34. Apple Bread

Preparation time: 5 minutes

Cooking time: 40 Minutes

Servings: 6

Ingredients:

- 3 cups apples
- 1 cup sugar
- 1 tablespoon. vanilla
- 2 eggs
- 1 tablespoon. apple pie spice
- 2 cups white flour
- 1 tablespoon. baking powder
- 1 stick butter
- 1 cup water

Directions:

1. Mix in egg with 1 butter stick, sugar, apple pie spice and turn using mixer.

2. Put apples and turn properly.

3. Mix baking powder with flour in another bowl and turn.

4. Blend the 2 mixtures, turn and move it to spring form pan.

5. Get spring form pan into air fryer and cook at 320°F for 40 minutes

6. Slice.

Nutrition: Calories: 401 Total Fat: 9g Total carbs: 29g

35. Banana Bread

Preparation time: 5 minutes

Cooking time: 40 Minutes

Servings: 6

Ingredients:

- ¾ cup sugar

- 1/3 cup butter

- 1 tablespoon. vanilla extract

- 1 egg

- 2 bananas

- 1 tablespoon. baking powder

- 1 and ½ cups flour

- ½ tablespoon. baking soda

- 1/3 cup milk

- 1 and ½ tablespoon. cream of tartar

- Cooking spray

Directions:

1. Mix in milk with cream of tartar, vanilla, egg, sugar, bananas and butter in a bowl and turn whole.

2. Mix in flour with baking soda and baking powder.

3. Blend the 2 mixtures, turn properly, move into oiled pan with cooking spray, put into air fryer and cook at 320°F for 40 minutes.

4. Remove bread, allow to cool, slice.

5. Serve.

Nutrition: Calories: 540 Total Fat: 16g Total carbs: 28g

36. Mini Lava Cakes

Preparation time: 5 minutes

Cooking time: 20 Minutes

Servings: 3

Ingredients:

- 1 egg

- 4 tablespoon. sugar

- 2 tablespoon. olive oil

- 4 tablespoon. milk

- 4 tablespoon. flour

- 1 tablespoon. cocoa powder

- ½ tablespoon. baking powder

- ½ tablespoon. orange zest

Directions:

1. Mix in egg with sugar, flour, salt, oil, milk, orange zest, baking powder and cocoa powder, turn properly. Move it to oiled ramekins. Put ramekins in air fryer and cook at 320°F for 20 minutes. Serve warm.

Nutrition: Calories: 329 Total Fat: 8.5g Total carbs: 12.4g

38. Cocoa Cookies

Preparation time: 10 minutes

Cooking time: 14 Minutes

Servings: 12

Ingredients:

- 6 oz. coconut oil

- 6 eggs

- 3 oz. cocoa powder

- 2 tablespoon. vanilla

- ½ tablespoon. baking powder

- 4 oz. cream cheese

- 5 tablespoon. sugar

Directions:

1. Mix in eggs with coconut oil, baking powder, cocoa powder, cream cheese, vanilla in a blender and sway and turn using a mixer. Get it into a lined baking dish and into the fryer at 320°F and bake for 14 minutes. Split cookie sheet into rectangles. Serve.

Nutrition: Calories: 149 Total Fat: 2.4g Total carbs: 27.2g

39. Special Brownies

Preparation time: 10 minutes

Cooking time: 22 Minutes

Servings: 4

Ingredients:

- 1 egg

- 1/3 cup cocoa powder

- 1/3 cup sugar

- 7 tablespoon. butter

- ½ tablespoon. vanilla extract

- ¼ cup white flour

- ¼ cup walnuts

- ½ tablespoon. baking powder

- 1 tablespoon. peanut butter

Directions:

1. Warm pan with 6 tablespoons butter and the sugar over medium heat, turn, cook for 5 minutes, move to a bowl, put salt, egg, cocoa powder, vanilla extract, walnuts, baking powder and flour, turn mix properly and into a pan.

2. Mix peanut butter with one tablespoon butter in a bowl, heat in microwave for some seconds, turn properly and sprinkle brownies blend over.

3. Put in air fryer and bake at 320° F and bake for 17 minutes.

4. Allow brownies to cool, cut.

5. Serve.

Nutrition: Calories: 438 Total Fat: 18g Total carbs: 16.5g

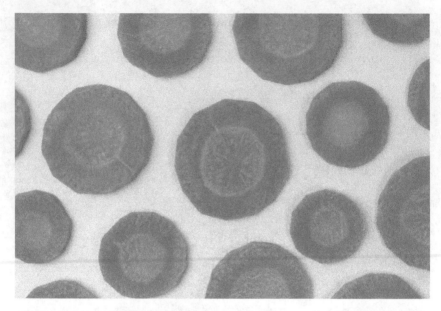

FAST FOOD

40. Chicken Spiedie Recipe

Preparation time: 10 minutes

Cooking time: 30 minutes

Servings: 4

Ingredients:

- 2 chicken breasts

- 1 large lemon

- 4 garlic cloves, thinly-sliced

- 1 tablespoon. basil

- 2 tablespoon. oregano

- Fresh mint

- Salt and ground black pepper to taste

- 1 tablespoon. olive oil

- Homemade bread rolls

- Homemade mayonnaise

- Skewers

Directions:

1. The first step is to marinate your chicken. To marinate, dice your chicken into big sized chunks and set them aside in a mixing bowl.

2. Squeeze the juice from the lemon into the same bowl, and the peeled and thinly-sliced garlic also. Then add seasoning and the olive oil.

3. Mix thoroughly with the hands and ensure the chicken is well coated. Now fill the skewers with the chicken and keep them in the fridge overnight.

4. The next step is to make the bread. Gather four bread rolls into the air fryer and allow them to cook at 365 F for 15 minutes.

5. Withdraw the cooked bread rolls and cook the chicken too, at 365 F for 15 minutes.

6. Fill the bread rolls with the stewed chicken, adding some homemade mayonnaise in the process.

7. Serve.

Nutrition: calories 503, fat 17, fiber 14.8, carbs 23, protein 43

SALAD RECIPES

41. Zucchini Salad

Preparation time: 15 minutes

Cooking Time: 30 minutes

Servings: 4

Ingredients:

- 1-pound zucchini, cut into rounds

- 2 tablespoons olive oil

- 1 teaspoon garlic powder

- Salt and ground black pepper, as required

- 5 cups fresh spinach, chopped

- ¼ cup feta cheese, crumbled

- 2 tablespoons fresh lemon juice

Directions:

1. Set the temperature of air fryer to 400 degrees F. Grease an air fryer basket.

2. In a bowl, mix together the zucchini, oil, garlic powder, salt, and black pepper.

3. Arrange zucchini slices into the prepared air fryer basket in a single layer.

4. Air fry for about 30 minutes, tossing 3 times.

5. Remove from air fryer and transfer the zucchini slices onto a plate.

6. Set aside to cool.

7. In another bowl, add the cooked zucchini slices, spinach, feta cheese, lemon juice, a little bit of salt, and black pepper and toss to coat well.

8. Serve immediately.

Nutrition: Calories: 116 Carbohydrate: 6.2g Protein: 4g Fat: 9.4g Sugar: 2.8g Sodium: 186mg

SNACK & APPETIZERS RECIPES

42. Sweet Potato Chips

Preparation Time: 10 minutes

Cooking Time: 20 minutes

Servings: 2

Ingredients:

- 1 medium sweet potato, sliced thinly

- 1/2 teaspoon ground cinnamon

- 2 tablespoon. olive oil

- Pepper

- Salt

Directions:

1. Soak sweet potato slices in cold water for 30 minutes. Drain well and pat dry.

2. Toss sweet potato slices with cinnamon, oil, pepper, and salt.

3. Place the dehydrating tray in a multi-level air fryer basket and place basket in the instant pot.

4. Arrange sweet potato slices on dehydrating tray.

5. Seal pot with air fryer lid and select air fry mode then set the temperature to 390 F and timer for 20 minutes. Turn halfway through.

6. Serve and enjoy.

Nutrition: Calories 173 Fat 14.1 g Carbohydrates 12.3 g Sugar 3.7 g Protein 1.2 g Cholesterol 0 mg

44. Spicy Chicken Wings

Preparation Time: 10 minutes

Cooking Time: 20 minutes

Servings: 2

Ingredients:

- 6 chicken wings

- 1 tablespoon. olive oil

- 1 teaspoon paprika

- Pepper

- Salt

Directions:

1. In a bowl, toss chicken wings, paprika, olive oil, pepper, and salt. Cover and place in the refrigerator for 1 hour.

2. Spray instant pot multi-level air fryer basket with cooking spray.

3. Add marinated chicken wings into the air fryer basket and place basket into the instant pot.

4. Seal pot with air fryer lid and select air fry mode then set the temperature to 390 F and timer for 20 minutes. Turn halfway through.

5. Serve and enjoy.

Nutrition: Calories 238 Fat 14 g Carbohydrates 0.6 g Sugar 0.1 g Protein 26.8 g Cholesterol 82 mg

45. Dry Rub Wings

Preparation Time: 10 minutes

Cooking Time: 14 minutes

Servings: 2

Ingredients:

- 8 chicken wings

- 1/2 teaspoon chili powder

- 1/2 teaspoon garlic powder

- 1/4 teaspoon pepper

- 1/4 teaspoon salt

Directions:

1. In a bowl, mix together chili powder, garlic powder, pepper, and salt.

2. Add chicken wings to the bowl and toss well.

3. Spray instant pot multi-level air fryer basket with cooking spray.

4. Add chicken wings into the air fryer basket and place basket into the instant pot.

5. Seal pot with air fryer lid and select air fry mode then set the temperature to 350 F and timer for 14 minutes. Turn halfway through.

6. Serve and enjoy.

Nutrition: Calories 242 Fat 9.4 g Carbohydrates 1 g Sugar 0.2 g Protein 36.3 g Cholesterol 111 mg

48. Indian Broccoli Florets

Preparation Time: 10 minutes

Cooking Time: 10 minutes

Servings: 2

Ingredients:

- 1 lb. broccoli florets

- 1/2 teaspoon chili powder

- 1/4 teaspoon turmeric powder

- 2 tablespoon. yogurt

- 1 tablespoon. chickpea flour

- 1/2 teaspoon salt

Directions

1. Add all ingredients to the bowl and toss well. Cover and place in the refrigerator for 20 minutes.

2. Spray instant pot multi-level air fryer basket with cooking spray.

3. Add marinated broccoli into the air fryer basket and place basket into the instant pot.

4. Seal pot with air fryer lid and select air fry mode then set the temperature to 390 F and timer for 10 minutes. Stir halfway through.

5. Serve and enjoy.

Nutrition: Calories 114 Fat 1.5 g Carbohydrates 20.5 g Sugar 5.7 g Protein 8.5 g Cholesterol 1 mg

49. Flavors Sweet Potato Wedges

Preparation Time: 10 minutes

Cooking Time: 20 minutes

Servings: 2

Ingredients:

- 2 sweet potatoes, cut into wedges

- 1 teaspoon cumin

- 1 tablespoon. Mexican seasoning

- 1 tablespoon. olive oil

- 1 teaspoon chili powder

- 1 teaspoon mustard powder

- Pepper

- Salt

Directions:

1. Add all ingredients into the bowl and toss well.

2. Spray instant pot multi-level air fryer basket with cooking spray.

3. Add potato wedges into the air fryer basket and place basket into the instant pot.

4. Seal pot with air fryer lid and select air fry mode then set the temperature to 350 F and timer for 20 minutes. Stir halfway through.

5. Serve and enjoy.

Nutrition: Calories 176 Fat 8.1 g Carbohydrates 24.9 g Sugar 0.6 g Protein 2.3 g Cholesterol 0 mg

50. Tasty Fishcake

Preparation Time: 10 minutes

Cooking Time: 15 minutes

Servings: 2

Ingredients:

- 1 1/2 cups white fish, cooked

- 1 tablespoon. butter

- 1/2 cup mashed potatoes

- 1 1/2 tablespoon. milk

- 1/2 teaspoon sage

- 1 teaspoon parsley

- 2 teaspoon flour

- Pepper

- Salt

Directions

1. Add all ingredients in a bowl and mix well.

2. Place the dehydrating tray in a multi-level air fryer basket and place basket in the instant pot.

3. Make patties and place on dehydrating tray.

4. Seal pot with air fryer lid and select air fry mode then set the temperature to 400 F and timer for 15 minutes. Turn patties halfway through.

5. Serve and enjoy.

Nutrition: Calories 442 Fat 37 g Carbohydrates 12.5 g Sugar 0.5 g Protein 15.9 g Cholesterol 17 mg

30 DAYS MEAL PLAN

Days	Breakfast	Snacks	Dinner
1	Sausage and Egg Breakfast Burrito	Eggplant Mix	Roasted Salmon with Lemon and Rosemary
2	Eggs in Avocado	Garlic Kale	Air Fried Meatballs with Parsley
3	French Toast Sticks	Herbed Tomatoes	Succulent Flank Steak
4	Home-Fried Potatoes	Coriander Potatoes	Chili Roasted Eggplant Soba
5	Homemade Cherry Breakfast Tarts	Tomatoes and Green beans	Quinoa and Spinach Cakes
6	Sausage and Cream Cheese Biscuits	Buttery Artichokes	Air Fried Cajun Shrimp
7	Fried Chicken and Waffles	Ginger Mushrooms	Air Fried Squid Rings
8	Cheesy Tater Tot Breakfast Bake	Masala Potatoes	Marinated Portobello Mushroom
9	Breakfast Scramble Casserole	Mixed Veggie Chips	Air Fried Meatloaf
10	Homemade Cherry Breakfast Tarts	Pear and Apple Chips	Fettuccini with Roasted Vegetables in Tomato Sauce
11	Mozzarella Tots	Banana and Cocoa Chips	Herbed Parmesan Turkey Meatballs
12	Chicken Balls	Roasted Chickpeas	Teriyaki Glazed Salmon and Vegetable Roast
13	Tofu Egg Scramble	Zucchini Chips	Sirloin with Garlic and Thyme
14	Flax & Hemp Porridge	Ranch Garlic Pretzels	Herbed Parmesan Turkey Meatballs

15	Creamy Bacon Eggs	Yellow Squash and Cream Cheese Fritters	Yogurt Garlic Chicken
16	Cheddar Bacon Hash	Air Fry Cheesy Taco Hot dogs	Lemony Parmesan Salmon
17	Cheddar Soufflé with Herbs	Crispy French Toast Sticks	Easiest Tuna Cobbler Ever
18	Bacon Butter Biscuits	Buttered Corn Cob	Deliciously Homemade Pork Buns
19	Keto Parmesan Frittata	Roasted Cashews	Mouthwatering Tuna Melts
20	Chicken Liver Pate	Panko Zucchini Fries	Bacon Wings
21	Coconut Pancake Hash	Rosemary Turnip Chips	Pepper Pesto Lamb
22	Beef Slices	Rosemary Carrot Fries	Tuna Spinach Casserole
23	Flax & Chia Porridge	Butternut Squash Fries	Greek Style Mini Burger Pies
24	Paprika Eggs with Bacon	Breaded Pickle Fries	Family Fun Pizza
25	Quiche Muffin Cups	Buttered Corn Cob	Crispy Hot Sauce Chicken
26	Easy Scotch Eggs	Polenta Bars	Herbed Parmesan Turkey Meatballs
27	Strawberry Toast	Eggplant Crisps	Sweet Potatoes & Creamy Crisp Chicken
28	Cinnamon Sweet-Potato Chips	Roasted Pecans	Mushroom & Chicken Noodles with Glasswort and Sesame
29	Quiche Muffin Cups	Crispy Broccoli Poppers	Prawn Chicken Drumettes
30	Vegetable and Ham Omelet	Potato Cheese Croquettes	Asian Popcorn Chicken

CONCLUSION

Regarding structure, an air fryer almost looks like a large rice cooker but with a front door handle. It has a removable chunky tray that holds the food to the air fried. It has an integrated timer to allow you to pre-set cooking times, and an adjustable temperature control so you can pre-set the best cooking temperature.

Different models offer different features, such as digital displays, auto-power shut-off, but mostly they work the same and use the same technology.

The air fryers have gained a lot of popularity over the last years due to their many advantages. Cooking in an air fryer is such a great and fun experience and you should try it as soon as possible.

The air fryer is such an innovative appliance that allows you to cook some of the best, most succulent and rich meals for you, your family and friends.

The air fryer reduces the cooking time and the effort you spend in the kitchen.

Having an air fryer is a great option. You can enjoy a healthier meal and save a good part of the oil expense, all without giving up enjoyable, fried foods.

Get a copy of this amazing air fryer cooking guide and use it to make real feast using this great appliance.

Start this culinary journey right away and enjoy the benefits of cooking with the air fryer.

CPSIA information can be obtained
at www.ICGtesting.com
Printed in the USA
BVHW090033280421
605944BV00005B/948